The Fine Art of Small Talk

Conversation Starters for Networking and Daily Life

Table of Contents

Introduction

I want to start this book by thanking and congratulating you for buying *The Fine Art of Small Talk: Conversation Starters for Networking and Daily Life.*

This book contains plenty of conversation starter tips and examples to help you initiate small talk with anyone, anytime, and anywhere. Ten seconds is all you will need to get someone interested in what you have to say, whether it be a person you've been dying to speak to at a party, an elderly person, a randomly encountered individual, or an old friend.

Keep in mind that moments of awkward silence are not worth fretting over. If, for instance, you find it challenging to know what to say whenever someone is left alone in a room with you, worry no more. With the coaching that is provided in this book, you will learn easy techniques to work around such situations.

With a handful of the techniques that are about to be shared with you in your back pocket, you are likely to be on your way to making new connections and saying goodbye to boredom.

I hope you enjoy!

Chapter 1 – Great Conversations Begin with Great Questions

"He explained to me with great insistence that every question possessed a power that did not lie in the answer."

- Elie Wiesel

All over the world, people of various cultures and languages use a common greeting that roughly translates into the following question: "How are you?" Remarkably, it is essentially globally understood that if you want to begin a conversation with someone, you must first ask a question. Therefore, it is our starting place as one of the most effective approaches to creating dialogue.

Tip # 1 – Ask a Question

Socrates, the great Greek philosopher, is known as the father of a brilliant method of questioning called Socratic questioning. He determined that you can use questions not only to get to the heart of ideas that may be difficult to understand, but also to aid in analysis and reveal what people really think about a particular topic. In fact, you may have even participated in Socratic circles or seminars in school whenever your teacher wanted you to dig deeper into a particular subject. Amazingly, students can grasps complex concepts just by sitting around and asking each other questions!

The basic application of Socrates' idea within the context of small talk is that once an open-ended question is put on the table, the person being addressed feels somehow obligated to throw back a response; they have to contribute to the conversation in an intelligent way. Whether your reason for engaging in this method of questioning with another person is to appear educated or to gather more information about a situation or even just to initiate small talk, it does not matter. It works. The next time you sense a conversation growing cold, why not heat it up with a little interrogation?

Loaded Points

If you start a discussion that you intend to steer in a particular direction, you will want to utilize leading questions. Ask a series of questions that leads the conversation to where you ultimately want it to go. Such inquiries allow the other person to elaborate on his ideas while giving you insight and direction on what to ask next. This method of questioning can be useful if you are trying to figure out a person's stance on something or if you want to subtly persuade someone to agree with your beliefs. Just be careful with the latter option, because when most people realize you are trying to dissuade them from believing a certain way through the use of persistent questioning, they can become defensive. This technique is typically used by reporters and journalists when they're trying to keep the subject of their interview on his toes. It is always best to use leading questions as a means to find out more about what a person thinks, and leave it at that.

Five Examples:

1. *"How has your experience in the university been so far?"*

2. *"What do you think about the statements the mayor dished to the public during the rally today?"*

3. *"Would you please fill me in on what you think of the government's new set of regulations?*

4. *"What do you plan on doing tomorrow?"*

5. *"What is your opinion regarding the topics at the national conference?"*

Recalls

Recalls are questions that require the other person to sift through their memories to highlight a specific event from the past. As recalls encourage active participation, they make great conversation starters. Some people may give simple responses to your queries, but most people typically love to reminisce about the past, so asking the right questions could get them rolling on a series of stories. With such people, you might find yourself making an altogether new memory of the time you swapped hilarious stories about deep-sea diving adventures for hours.

Five Examples:

1. *"What is jumping off a cliff like?"*
2. *"What was your first dog's name?"*
3. *"What was the first concert you attended?*
4. *"Who was your first violin teacher?"*
5. *"Why weren't you at the palace for your friend's birthday party?"*

The Rhetorical Way

Another way to begin making small talk is by unleashing some rhetorical questions. These are humorous points that incline the person you are talking to, to share his five cents worth. He may want to throw an equally witty comeback at you or he may end up contemplating what you've said to have a legitimate discussion. Just beware that in most cases, these clever quips can come across as being irritating to some people. If you use them recklessly, you may find yourself in the midst of a feud. Rhetorical questions are best used within the context of the conversation at hand and sparingly.

Five Examples:

1. *"If you are asleep, how are you aware of it?"*

2. *"If the stars are bright, why is it still dark at night?"*

3. *"If you find yourself, are you another individual?"*

4. *"When you cry, will your tears run out?"*

5. *"If he jumps off that ledge, won't he break something?"*

The YES or NO Method

Questions that require nothing but YES or NO answers are called closed end questions. They are excellent conversation starters in situations involving a withdrawn participant. By employing the use of a closed end question, it does not matter whether or not the other person is apt to get into a discussion with you. Only one word is required to respond: YES or NO. Rather than forcing him to give a lengthy response, you give him the privilege of making a choice. If he wants to expand on his answer, it is up to him to do so; if he does not, it is all good.

Five Examples:

1. *"Are you going to do the marathon next year?"*

2. *"Did you finish your meal?"*

3. *"Is it three o'clock already?"*

4. *"Have you bought a gift for your nephew's party yet?"*

5. *"Were you the one I spotted at the mall yesterday?"*

It may be beneficial for you to go back through each of these categories and construct your own set of questions. You can do it as an exercise to expand your conversational creativity or you can do it as preparation before you attend an event where you know you will have to meet new people. The more you practice each form of questioning, the better you will get at them, and the more natural you will sound when you use them. It is always best to *listen* to what someone is saying and make sure your question is delivered within the right context, but it is also good to prepare yourself beforehand.

Chapter 2 – Themed Gatherings

"What is there more kindly than the feeling between host and guest?"

- Aeschylus

Whenever people come together for a party or special event, it is always an opportunity in the making for new connections. Extroverts and introverts alike enter the door with similar expectations. They want to have a good time. Though people attend parties for various reasons, getting the chance to engage in great conversations is one of the things people will remember most about your party when they reflect on it months or even years later, so give them something worth remembering!

Tip # 2 – Be an Incredible Host

If you can recall the best party you've ever attended, chances are that the party's host is a vivid part of your memory. Whether she was mingling with the guests and cracking jokes with everyone or she was constantly shifting gears and introducing new games or topics of conversation, she took her job as the host seriously. Believe it or not, but when people attend a party at your place, they will view the event as an extension of your personality. If the party is boring, they assume you are equally boring. That's why when inviting family, friends, and co-workers to a party at your place, you should make it your utmost responsibility to keep them entertained.

One great way to prepare for a party is to ensure that you have plenty of conversation starters on hand. If you are having a small dinner party, it might be nice to keep a bunch of conversation starters in your back pocket to get everyone talking at the dinner table. If the gathering is larger, you can pre-plan some ideas for how to engage guests one at a time or in small groups. Your guests are counting on you to keep an eye out for their overall excitement level. If you do not, they will not only regret having attended your affair, but the next time you call them to join you for another celebration, they will think twice before agreeing or maybe even refuse to show up at all.

A Battle of Favorites

One of the best methods you can use to hit it off with guests at a party is to get them talking about things they're passionate about. Politics, sports, civil rights, television shows and movies are all general topics that can touch a multitude of interests. If you steer the conversation towards something a person is passionate about, it won't matter if they're the most introverted person in the room, they will talk... a lot. After a word or phrase they're familiar with is mentioned, you will visibly be able to tell that you've piqued their interest, because they'll turn to face you and listen intently to what you are saying. You've got their full attention. In such a case, using this method is likely to incite the start of a lengthy conversation, which may turn into a budding friendship.

Five Examples:

1. *"I like your argyle sweater. I wear argyle sweaters all the time."*

2. *"Have you heard of Angels & Airwaves? It's my favorite group."*

3. *"I love that episode where Mr. White first met Saul Goodman."*

4. *"I enjoy gardening. What do you like to do in your free time?"*

5. *"So you're a Trekkie too. Captain Jean Luc Picard is my hero."*

Everybody Loves to Eat

Since many people adore food, why not initiate small talk over some of the special cuisine you prepared or ordered? Guests will appreciate the fact that apart from keeping them occupied, you are also occupying their taste buds. There's something about eating food while fellowshipping with friends that increases the enjoyment factor for people. Think about ice cream or any other type of comfort food. Why do people tend to eat them when they're depressed? Because they work wonders to soothe the soul. If you plan such foods for your party, you will subtly be aiding in the contentment of your guests.

On top of that, if your food is any good, you will undoubtedly have people that will be interested in getting your recipes. One of the biggest items you see circulating on social media today is recipes. You can not only use some of those recipes to treat your guests, but you can use their interest in the recipe to get connected with them online as you share the link with them. Depending on how into cooking you and your guests are, you might even end up swapping recipes or stories about great food experiences in various restaurants.

Five Examples:

1. *"Here, you have to try a slice of this strawberry cake. It is amazing!"*

2. *"I got the recipe from an Italian friend who's so into pasta."*

3. *"One time I ordered one of those jumbo burgers at a local diner, and I loved it. That's what I was aiming for with these. You should try one."*

4. *"This one's a delicacy in Asian countries."*

5. *"I've always preferred Mexican specialties. I actually got this recipe when I went to Acapulco for spring break last year."*

Random Throws

To catch people's attention at a party or to simply catch them off guard and shake things up a bit, try showing your spontaneous side in a sort of "So... how 'bout them Cowboys?" kind of way. You could randomly begin discussing the regulations at your workplace or talk about a typical day in France or even blurt out the lyrics to a bizarre song. Because the point is to be random, the topic of choice is totally up to you. Random throws can be extremely helpful when you need to change the subject, especially if things get tense or awkward, but like rhetorical questions, they must be strategically placed.

Five Examples:

1. *"Did you hear about the dogs that were provided mini mansions by a billionaire?"*

2. *"If I could go anywhere, I'd be at a beach in Thailand in a heartbeat."*

3. *"Some people mistake astronomy for astrology; they think that the job of an astronomer involves reading horoscopes."*

4. *"Did you know most retailers have equipment meant to assist in folding clothes?"*

5. *"You can make poison out of beans."*

Before inviting people to a gathering of any sort, mentally sort through each individual that will be in attendance (if the number is small enough), and note each person's passions and interests. Be sure to make each person feel welcome and appreciated by greeting them personally and engaging in meaningful conversation with them. It may be of interest to you to do a little research beforehand, if you know half of the attendees are into hockey and you know nothing about the sport.

Also, remember to present food that is out of the box if you intend to have out of the box conversations. Provide the kind of food that will get people talking! Have you ever seen those commercials where they show the difference between two parties that serve two different snacks? It is not just creative advertising; it is the truth. Food makes all the difference in social gatherings. People simply enjoy themselves more when they enjoy the food.

But even with all your pre-party planning, do not forget to allow some room to practice a little bit of spontaneity. You might be the life of your own party!

Chapter 3 – For That Special Someone

"A conversation with a special person may turn out beautifully."

- Mandy Hale

We all have certain people in our lives that intrigue us. Maybe your special someone has a captivating personality or charm, or maybe it is his looks that have captured your attention. Whatever the reason for attraction may be, all you know is that you'd really like to get to know him. Sometimes having such feelings can cause nerves – better known as butterflies – to hinder your ability to keep a conversation going, but they do not have to.

Many a movie has poked fun at the way people trip over themselves verbally and sometimes even physically, when they're nervous about meeting someone. It is humorous to watch, but it is not so humorous when it is happening to you. It can actually be quite frustrating. The easiest way to get over the butterflies is to simply go for it. There's nothing you can do to get rid of them entirely, so you have to let them run their course. Just take a deep breath, remind yourself how important getting to know this person is, and resolve not to let nerves make you miss out on the possibility of a new relationship. Maybe one day you will both look back and laugh about the funny situations your nerves got you into when you first spoke to each other.

Tip # 3 – Go Out of Your Way

Are you used to being approached by people instead of approaching them? If you want to begin a relationship with someone special, you have to be ready to go out of your way to start a conversation with him. Flip things around for once and approach him first! To seek someone out just to engage in conversation with him demonstrates a high level of interest on your part just like avoiding someone shows a high level of disinterest. The simple fact that you chose to reach out first will speak volumes to your special friend. Everyone likes to feel wanted, and your pursuit of him will demonstrate just that.

While you are at it, once you find out what activities mean a lot to him, consider engaging in them yourself. It will give you something that he's interested in to talk about, and as you read earlier, you can have great conversations with people when you get them talking about their passions. Make sure that you do not lose yourself in the process of trying to get someone's attention though. The point of getting involved in his favorite activities is simply to show that what's important to him is important to you, not to give yourself a personality overhaul. Even so, in the end, the bonus of it all is that stepping outside of your comfort zone is likely to raise your chances of impressing him.

Be Thoughtful

A great way to start a conversation with someone special is to be thoughtful. Try reminding him in unique ways that he's valued. Even if he does not seem to think he's done anything to merit your words of affirmation, aim to brighten his day anyway. These thoughtful comments can be coupled with kind gestures as well (e.g. a token of appreciation, an object that will be helpful to him at work or home, etc.). If he's had a rough day, your glimmer of kindness will especially work wonders to cheer him up. Be careful not to lay it on too thick as that can come across as being a bit overbearing, and in some cases creepy, but do not be afraid to make sure that he feels like his life matters.

Five Examples:

1. *"Happy Birthday! I hope you have the best one yet."*

2. *"How are you feeling today? I've been thinking about you this morning."*

3. *"I bought two boxes of cupcakes today; one for me and one for you."*

4. *"I can help you water your plants today."*

5. *"I've noticed you working really hard on the house. Are you thirsty? I've brought you a bottle of water."*

Getting Personal

If you consider someone to be special, show him that he means something to you by getting personal with him – especially if a close relationship is what you are after. There's something in our human nature that makes us feel at ease enough to share our personal feelings when someone else does it first, so why not make the effort to initiate a meaningful conversation by handing over a bit of personal information about yourself? Do not be afraid to extend a portion of who you are to him. In most cases, you won't regret it. Just do not get too personal too fast. Ease your way into it.

You can even probe him for personal information by sharing things you've noticed about the way he acts, dresses, speaks, etc. Being observant and noting little details that most people would overlook is also a great way to help him see that you really care about him. When you open up and share more about yourself and point out interesting tidbits you've noticed about him, eventually, your discussions will give you a much clearer sense of who the person across from you really is.

Five Examples:

1. *"I was very close with my brother, growing up. We were the only two kids in my family. How many siblings do you have?"*

2. *"I haven't ever seen you drink soda. Is there a reason behind that?"*

3. *"I often see you at the library on Tuesdays. I usually go there to study with my friend, but you are always on your own. Do you prefer it that way?"*

4. *"When I was little, I wanted to work for NASA. How about you? What did you want to be?"*

5. *"You always wear a red shirt every 15th of the month. Perhaps there's some significance to it."*

I'm Into That Too

Try making small talk by bringing up a mutual interest. The more you have in common, the better the connection, so look for common interests and start there. If he's into poetry and you happen to be into it too, engage him in discussions regarding the lives of your favorite poets and share lines from your favorite poems with each other. If you are aware that the he's a fan of particular band, show that you either have knowledge about the band or at least show that you could get into their music if he introduced you to them. You do not have to be interested in the exact same things, but it helps to show that you could be interested if given the chance.

Five Examples:

1. *"I think I might be as fond of blueberry cheesecake as you are."*

2. *"I could spend hours staring at paintings in art galleries too."*

3. *"I've watched the Lord of the Rings trilogy at least three times; I'm well on my way to match your record of seven."*

4. *"Just like you, I fancy minimal designs. Less is more, right?"*

5. *"I cannot stop listening to Kings of Leon either!"*

Words of Wisdom

If your loved one is more of the straightforward, realistic type who likes people to tell it to him like it is and cringes whenever he's given a dose of optimism that he feels is insincere, you may want to bypass the fluffy stuff and just call things like you see them. He'll appreciate your approach and will equally appreciate your presence. Start a conversation with him on a raw yet insightful note. Be honest, but be kind. No one wants to feel berated. Though some people love hearing positive words to make them feel better when they're going through a tough time, many people prefer inspiring but honest exchanges. It is important that you determine which one of these people your special person is.

Five Examples:

1. *"If you approach this with a lazy attitude, you shouldn't be surprised if your colleague is promoted, because he consistently works hard."*

2. *"It's all right to feel bad that you didn't reach your boss' standards. Just remind yourself that sometimes you can't please people and it's on you if you let that fact bother you."*

3. *"I've failed the test numerous times myself. You'll get it. Later on, you'll look back on today and laugh."*

4. *"Not all feats in life are achievable. If you aren't successful at something, it's okay to cut yourself some slack."*

5. *"You seem to perform better when you're on your own than when you are with a team. Keep it up. When you have a vision in mind, you are good about making sure it is accomplished."*

Every individual is unique, and they like to be treated as such. Therefore, as this section states, the most important factor in starting a conversation with someone special to you is to do all you can to learn who he is and what he is into. You can do that by being the first one to get a little vulnerable to make him feel at ease enough to share, and you can also do it by getting him to talk in depth about whatever is most important to him. Listen intently to what he has to say, learn from it, and then between that conversation and the next time you see him, you can do a little research or come up with a small gesture to impress him with how much you know about his interests.

Chapter 4 – On the Internet

"The internet is just a world passing around notes in a classroom."

- Jon Stewart

One of the beauties of the World Wide Web is that you can not only easily stay informed of how your friends are doing, but you have a fairly constant open line of communication with them – especially if they're avid Smartphone users. The Internet has changed the face of what friendship looks like in this day in age, but just because it is different does not mean that it does not work or it is not good. In the case of long distance relationships, communication via the Internet is nearly essential. Even though there are many campaigns circulating on social media these days to get people to spend less time on their phones and more time with people, online communication can be a great supplement to building lasting relationships.

Tip # 4 – Do not Close Your Doors on Strangers

When you hardly (or maybe never) see your buddy, it does not take long for the two of you to become estranged. Typically, as time rolls on and people change, topics of conversation get harder and harder to find, and both parties eventually get disinterested in putting forth the effort to maintain the relationship. You may have experienced this with friends in schools, in previous cities you've lived in, or at old workplaces. A change in location also brings a change in friends, but the one thing that does not change with your old friends is your friendship status online.

Whenever you spot an old friend online, take a moment to check in on her. Ask her about her day. Get an update on what has happened in her life since the last time you spoke. Let her know that even though you have not spoken to her in a while, you are still interested in their wellbeing. Perhaps you can set up a time for the two of you to meet. Many relationships that once were considered to have been phased out were renewed simply because small talk online opened up the door for further conversation. The Internet can be a great tool to remind people, even in small ways, that you are still around and you still care.

Being Polite

In the case that your online pal has expressed his views on a certain topic, and you vehemently disagree with them, remember to be polite and stay objective. Refrain from posting aggressive remarks or passive aggressive statuses. One negative aspect of social media is that people often use it as a digital journal. When someone is upset about something, they go to Facebook to vent. Some people tend to believe that they can get away with posting passive aggressive statuses about friends, but the truth is that the person you are talking about always knows that you are talking about them, and they take it to heart. Your comments online can ruin a friendship that otherwise could have easily been mended. So instead of flying off the handle, remain even-tempered, try to accept the fact that not everybody thinks alike, and let him know you will take his opinion into consideration.

Five Examples:

1. *"I disagree with your opinion on marriages. In contrast to what you said, I believe that it is the husband and wife that are responsible for their own bond; others hardly play a role."*

2. *"I respect your view, although I have my own."*

3. *"I think there's another approach. Yours is good but perhaps less people will be affected if we try it this way instead."*

4. *"Most of the students, myself included, do not like your idea. I hope we all can come to an understanding.*

5. *"Thank you for the advice; however, I'm not in agreement with what you are promoting."*

Give Out a Bunch of Compliments

Do not overlook the fact that your friend's day will be made when she receives a delightful word from you. For instance, if she has just posted a new profile picture on Facebook. Do not just ignore it. People change their profile pictures not for their own sake, but because they want other people to express their approval and admiration. When you change your profile picture, what is your expectation from your friends. It is likely that their expectation is not too different from your own. In that wise, you may want to hit the *Like* button (that is if you actually like her picture) and tell her how great she looks.

Five Examples:

1. *"I'm totally a fan of your blog. I read it every chance that I get."*

2. *"I like how you're always at ease during crazy days like today."*

3. *"That sweater you're wearing is nice. Where did you buy it?"*

4. *"You're a genius! People who want site errors fixed quickly should come to you."*

5. *"Your post is insightful and witty. Great job."*

Just Say It

Social media is ripe with opportunities to make small talk. When people post statuses, they're usually not looking to have long, drawn out conversations; just a little back forth. Take advantage of the opportunity to make small talk and play along. You can post an encouraging word or share your opinion, or you can even utilize some of the question techniques outlined earlier. If the person is a fan of a movie character, for instance, and he's dying for just one soul to understand his fondness for a certain film, he'll appreciate your initiative to ask questions or agree with his statement. Chances are, if your comment on his status leads you to discover that you have something in common, you will become best buddies in the long run.

Five Examples:

1. *"I know, right? No one really reads the terms of services anyway."*

2. *"I watch Pretty Little Liars too. I cannot believe Maya would do such a thing."*

3. *"Me neither. I cannot make any sense of the senator's campaign. He has way too many initiatives to promote."*

4. *"Tell me about it. Cats are rather messy."*

5. *"Thank you for pointing that out. It infuriates me how some people complain about things they can totally control themselves."*

Truthfully, of all the forms of small talk listed in this book, communication through the Internet is the easiest. If you are already online and you happen to come across your friend's profile, all you have to do is shoot them a quick hello, and then the ball is in their court. You do not have to force the conversation or scramble for topics to talk about; you just wait until they reply (if they reply), and pick it up from there.

Though some people would claim that conversations via the Internet are a lesser form of communication or that they take away from *real* relationships, it is important to remember that regardless of the medium through which you communicate, you are communicating with people, and people like to feel important, appreciated, and valued. Utilize whatever opportunity you may have to do that, even if it comes in the form of a *Like, and j*ust be a friend regardless of the context.

Chapter 5 – Especially for the Elderly

"The best classroom in the world is at the feet of an elderly person."

- Andy Rooney

Though we live in the information age, and we typically prefer to get information about current and past events online, there is no better source than the people who were around when the events were happening. We live in a day and age where this select group is largely ignored rather than adored, but they have very valuable information to share, and for the most part they would love to be able to share it with you.

Tip # 5 – Be Accommodating

For someone who grew up in the forties or fifties, today's culture can be a bit shocking. The language is different, the clothing is different, and the general attitude of young people is very different. Things were much simpler in their days, so the rapid pace and technological slant of this day and age can really frustrate them. Generally speaking, the older people get, the less willing they are to embrace change. In fact, they may be very vocal about their disdain of the young generation and their desire for things to be the way they used to be. It can be very off-putting at first.

When you are trying to accommodate folks more than twenty years older than you, give them plenty of space to share their perspective and give lots of positive feedback. Remember to choose your words wisely. A kind word will always go much farther when engaging in dialogue with an elderly person. They do not like to babied or treated like a child, but they do appreciate your respect. They like to know that they still have a voice and that you *heard* them. Elderly people have loads of exciting experiences to share and can be fun to have conversations with, even if they can be quite a handful at times.

Current Events

The latest happenings are brilliant conversation starters to get the elderly to give you their undivided attention. They typically have no interest in trivial conversations and prefer to focus on things that matter the most to them, so make sure that the words that come out of your mouth are informative. Have you heard the saying that history repeats itself? Well, it does, and if you take a moment to chat with an older person about what is happening in the world, you will discover that they have a lot of insight on the subject simply because they have lived through it before. Having a conversation with someone who has "been there and done that" can actually save you a lot of grief in the long-run, if actually pay attention to what they have to say.

Five Examples:

1. *"Have you read about the medical breakthrough in stem cell therapy?"*

2. *"I've read the story of a young boy being reunited with his mother after they had lost touch with each other for almost a decade."*

3. *"The stock market does not seem to be doing too well these days."*

4. *"The other day, a politician was imprisoned for his corrupt ways."*

5. *"The weather seems nice. According to news reports though, it's not going to stay this way as a storm is approaching."*

R-E-S-P-E-C-T

As was mentioned before, because older people have been around longer, they typically have a lot to say. To some people, the elderly might come across as know-it-alls. They think they have answer for everything, and they want everyone to know it. It can almost make you regret ever having started a conversation with them. There is really only a small subset of the elderly population that behaves that way, so try not to over-generalize and assume they all are like that.

The truth is that they are just acting by a moral code that was established thousands of years ago: respect your elders. Sadly, people today have really lost sight of this particular cultural expectation, and the elderly have found themselves at the bottom of the totem pole for respect. So if they seem to demand your respect, it is only because that is all they know. If you are the kind of person who does not like being instructed by other people, it may be tempting to forget your manners and tell them what you really think about their archaic ideas, but you must remember to keep in mind how important it is for them to able to speak up too.

Five Examples:

1. *"I'm not sure I understand your reasons right now, but I trust that it worked for you, so I will give the matter some more thought."*

2. *"For me, this technique has been the most effective. Don't worry though - I will gladly try yours some time."*

3. *"I do not agree with orthodox methods, but since you've brought it up, I will take some time to look it up."*

4. *"It's all right. Even though it's giving me a hard time right now, this is more convenient for me."*

5. *"Your method seems effective, but I think I find it easier to go at it another way. Thanks, though."*

Time for Some Self-Appreciation

When dealing with an elderly person, spare some time to talk about yourself. Yes, they have a lot to say about what is going on in the world, but they also have in interest in the person they are talking to. That would be another aspect you can attribute to their upbringing. Relationship is key. After getting acquainted with each other, do not hesitate to share more about your life. They may find what you are up to amusing, or as you share your background, you may find that two of you have certain people or places in common. Given the breadth of most senior citizens' life experiences, sharing your interests could be the jumping off point for some really interesting stories.

Five Examples:

1. *"I go to church every Saturday and I play the guitar."*

2. *"I once had a pet lemur whose name was Miguel."*

3. *"I plan to go to India in the summer. It will be my fifth country to visit in the last two years."*

4. *"On weekends, I spend my time bowling with friends."*

5. *"When I'm listening to music, I find it disturbing to have other people in the room with me."*

In the end, there's a lot that both sides of the equation can glean from each other. Sometimes if the elderly person is immobile, they actually like to connect with people that are mobile so they can live vicariously through them. In such cases they may even ask more questions about what you are up to than share about their own life. The important thing is to be open to giving *and* receiving. Even if you do not feel you have much in common with the person, you can believe that the mere fact that you took time out to speak with him made his day a little bit brighter.

Chapter 6 – Friends for Keeps

"To cultivate friendship, it's to hang in, stay connected."

- Jon Katz

When you have a close bond with a friend, it doesn't matter the time you've spent apart or the distance, you can pick up where you left off like it was just yesterday. Friendships like that are hard to come by because they have to be cultivated. They do not just happen overnight! In fact, of all the friends you have, it is very likely that less than a handful of them would fit in this category. You may have a lot of friends, but you only have a few forever friends.

Tip # 6 – Cherish Memories

Usually, after spending years apart from friends that you used to be really close to, it can be difficult to get a conversation started. You used to finish each other's sentences, but getting back to that level of synchronicity may take a little work. If you have even the slightest inkling of a thought that says, *I wish things could be the way they used to be,* it is important that you refuse to let the bonds of friendship die and that you search for that unity that was once there. If you feel the friendship is a lifelong one, remember you are the one that has to make that a reality.

Catching Up

As you've been absent in each other's lives for a while, it would be wise to initiate small talk to not only catch up, but to feel things out a bit. The person you knew previously may not be the person standing in front of you or on the other end of the phone. You must be careful not to treat your friend as the person she once was, but to seek to discover who she has become. Let her know that even if you have less in common than you used to, that you value her friendship. Relating with an old friend on these terms is among one of the best ways to hit it off again.

Five Examples:

1. *"How do you spend your free time these days?"*

2. *"Do you still like to read poems about swans? I still have the ones you gave me. I put them in my treasure box."*

3. *"How is your family? Is your mom still living in the West Coast?*

4. *"What are you up to nowadays?"*

5. *"Where are you working now?"*

Remember When...

Recalling moments the two of you once deemed unforgettable can be a great conversation starter as well. As you and your friend are connected by a number of mutual events, chances are high that many entertaining discussions will flare up. Consider inviting your friend to meet you a particular spot you both used to frequent: a local coffee shop, a nearby park, etc. The environment you choose will play a huge role in sparking memories and making the two of you feel at ease. In such a setting you can easily interchange memories of old with stories of what is new. Apart from feeling nostalgic, you will be reminded of the kind of enjoyment you were privileged to have before, as you look ahead to what will unfold.

Five Examples:

1. *"Do you remember when we used to hang out all the time at that grocery store around the corner?"*

2. *"I still have the shirt I wore when our group went to that music festival."*

3. *"I was always envious of the blanket forts you made when we were kids. Mine never lasted through the night."*

4. *"Our high school classmate Harry once went berserk after news got to him that his best friend Tim went the other way."*

5. *"I miss the summer days we spent in our rollerblades."*

The test of time proves how strong a friendship is, but it also determines how diligent you are in ensuring that the flame of friendship does not simmer down to a flicker. If you want the relationship to continue, you have to acknowledge that there may be an awkward phase when you first reconnect, but then you have to commit to working towards getting past it. The awkward stage could last for minutes, days, or even weeks, but with some persistence, you will soon begin to feel the warmth of your old friendship slowly begin to permeate your conversation.

If you have some friends that you haven't spoken to in a while, take some time to contact them and get the conversation between you two going again. What begins as small talk can quickly evolve into an intense dialogue, just like the old days.

Conclusion

Thank you again for buying ***The Fine Art of Small Talk: Conversation Starters for Networking and Daily Life.***

After leafing through all six chapters, you should have a gained pretty good understanding of how to hit it off with any person you encounter. From this point on, consider using the tips and examples shared with you. You may even create a similar bunch of conversation starters of your own based on what you've learned or create new categories of your own. However you plan to proceed is totally up to you.

If you enjoyed this book, you may want to take the time to share your thoughts in the form of a review on Amazon. Tell others of your experiences too. Also, why not recommend this book to a friend? Especially if you have that buddy who cannot seem to get past his fright of initiating a discussion with others, try extending help. Remind him that he's got all the techniques here to show him the way; no longer does he have to be burdened by awkward silence.

Thank you and good luck!

Check Out My Other Kindle Books

Evernote for Your Productivity - The Beginner's Guide to Getting Things Done with Evernote or How to Organize Your Life with Notetaking and Archiving

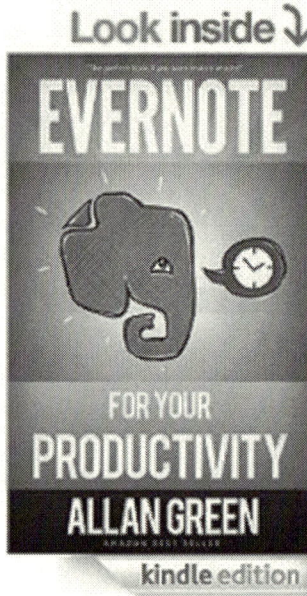

Download link: **http://amzn.to/1EI3zjD**

Or just search for the title of the book and you will find the book by Allan Green.

1) Resume Writing for IT Professionals - Resume Magic or How to Find a Job with Resumes and Cover Letters

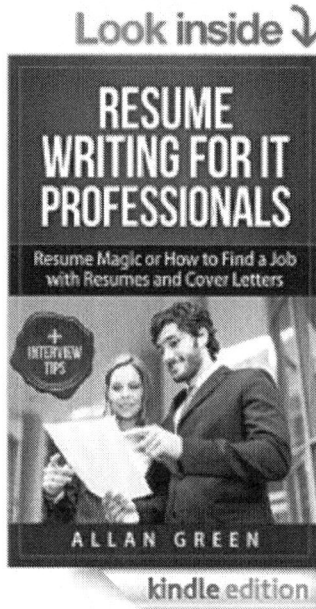

Download link: **http://amzn.to/1JWsgZz**

Or just search for the title of the book and you will find the book by Allan Green.

2) Leadership Skills: Guide to Developing Leadership Skills or 7 Habits of the Leader in Me

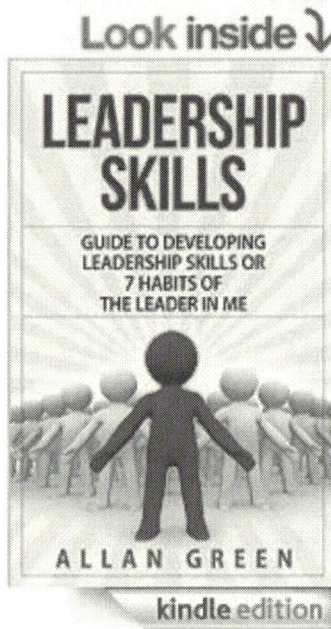

Download link: **http://amzn.to/1Q6hFPF**

Or just search for the title of the book and you will find the book by Allan Green.

3) Your Speed Reading Guide - How to Increase Reading Speed and Read Faster, Productivity Improvement Book

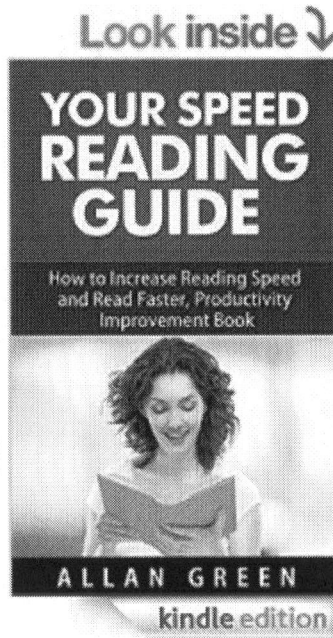

Download link: **http://amzn.to/1c1HFgC**

Or just search for the title of the book and you will find the book by Allan Green.

4) Why 90% of Startups FAIL? - Starting Small Business for Dummies, Entrepreneur Books

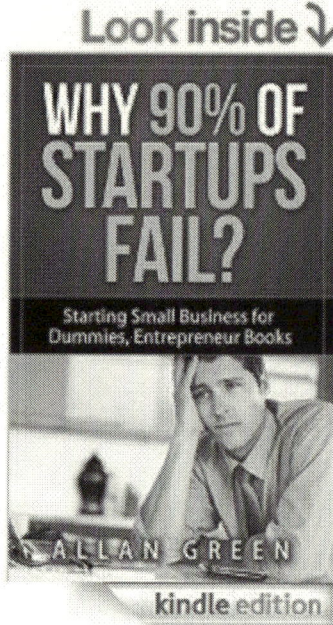

Download link: **http://amzn.to/1Je2Q9A**

Or just search for the title of the book and you will find the book by Allan Green.

5) The Key To Positive Thinking - How to Be Happy and Think Positive, A Happiness Project Book

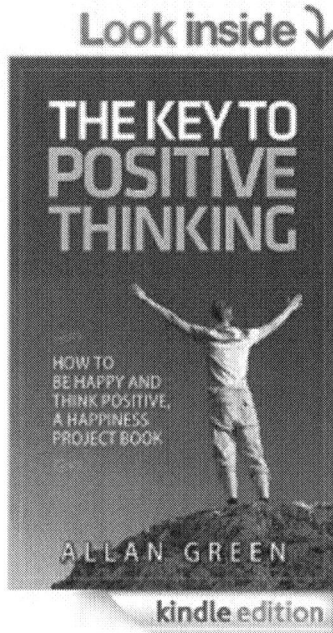

Download link: **http://amzn.to/1EVnPQR**

Or just search for the title of the book and you will find the book by Allan Green.

6) Self-Confidence - How to Build Confidence and Master Conflict Management Skills

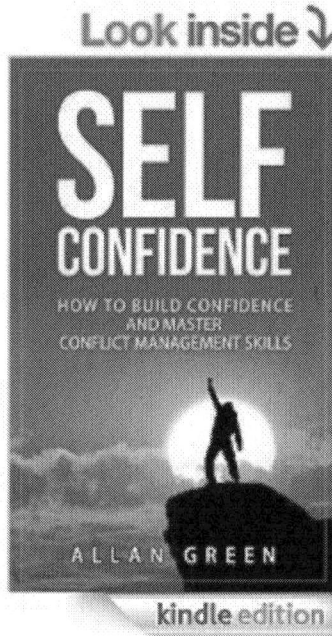

Download link: **http://amzn.to/1AoVQBK**

Or just search for the title of the book and you will find the book by Allan Green.

33018034R00032